# HOME MAINTENANCE
## LOG BOOK

—THIS BOOK BELONGS TO—

Name : ------------------------------------------

Address : ----------------------------------------

---------------------------------------------

| PROFESSIONAL NAME | PHONE | COMPANY NAME |
| --- | --- | --- |
| Electrician | | |
| Plumber | | |
| HAVC | | |
| Roofer | | |
| Handyman | | |
| Lawncare | | |
| Sprinkler System | | |
| Pool | | |
| Hardscapes | | |
| Windos/Siding | | |
| Homewners Insurance | | |
| Homewners System | | |
| Police | | |
| Fire | | |
| Trash Removal | | |
| Recycling | | |
| Phone/Cable/Satellite | | |
| Homewners Association | | |
| Village/Township | | |
| Voting Precinct | | |

Notes :

# Important *Contacts*

| PROFESSIONAL NAME | PHONE | COMPANY NAME |
|---|---|---|
| Electrician | | |
| Plumber | | |
| HAVC | | |
| Roofer | | |
| Handyman | | |
| Lawncare | | |
| Sprinkler System | | |
| Pool | | |
| Hardscapes | | |
| Windos/Siding | | |
| Homewners Insurance | | |
| Homewners System | | |
| Police | | |
| Fire | | |
| Trash Removal | | |
| Recycling | | |
| Phone/Cable/Satellite | | |
| Homewners Association | | |
| Village/Township | | |
| Voting Precinct | | |

Notes :

# Important *Contacts*

| PROFESSIONAL NAME | PHONE | COMPANY NAME |
| --- | --- | --- |
| Electrician | | |
| Plumber | | |
| HAVC | | |
| Roofer | | |
| Handyman | | |
| Lawncare | | |
| Sprinkler System | | |
| Pool | | |
| Hardscapes | | |
| Windos/Siding | | |
| Homewners Insurance | | |
| Homewners System | | |
| Police | | |
| Fire | | |
| Trash Removal | | |
| Recycling | | |
| Phone/Cable/Satellite | | |
| Homewners Association | | |
| Village/Township | | |
| Voting Precinct | | |

Notes :

# Important *Contacts*

| PROFESSIONAL NAME | PHONE | COMPANY NAME |
|---|---|---|
| Electrician | | |
| Plumber | | |
| HAVC | | |
| Roofer | | |
| Handyman | | |
| Lawncare | | |
| Sprinkler System | | |
| Pool | | |
| Hardscapes | | |
| Windos/Siding | | |
| Homewners Insurance | | |
| Homewners System | | |
| Police | | |
| Fire | | |
| Trash Removal | | |
| Recycling | | |
| Phone/Cable/Satellite | | |
| Homewners Association | | |
| Village/Township | | |
| Voting Precinct | | |

Notes :

# Home Maintenance *Calender*

## JANUARY

## FEBRUARY

## MARCH

## APRIL

## MAY

## JUN

## JULY

## AUGUST

## SEPTEMBER

## OCTOBER

## NOVEMBER

## DECEMBER

# Where *it is?*

| Water Heater | Electrical Box |
|---|---|
| | |

| Hvac Units | Water Meter & Min Shut-off |
|---|---|
| | |

| Gas Meter & Maib Shut-Off | Sprinkler Controls |
|---|---|
| | |

| Smoke Detectors | Fire Extinguishers |
|---|---|
| | |

# Where *it is?*

## Water Heater

## Electrical Box

## Hvac Units

## Water Meter & Min Shut-off

## Gas Meter & Maib Shut-Off

## Sprinkler Controls

## Smoke Detectors

## Fire Extinguishers

# Where *it is?*

| Water Heater | Electrical Box |
|:---:|:---:|
| | |

| Hvac Units | Water Meter & Min Shut-off |
|:---:|:---:|
| | |

| Gas Meter & Maib Shut-Off | Sprinkler Controls |
|:---:|:---:|
| | |

| Smoke Detectors | Fire Extinguishers |
|:---:|:---:|
| | |

# Where *it is?*

## Water Heater

## Electrical Box

## Hvac Units

## Water Meter & Min Shut-off

## Gas Meter & Maib Shut-Off

## Sprinkler Controls

## Smoke Detectors

## Fire Extinguishers

# Where *it is?*

| Water Heater | Electrical Box |
| --- | --- |
| | |

| Hvac Units | Water Meter & Min Shut-off |
| --- | --- |
| | |

| Gas Meter & Maib Shut-Off | Sprinkler Controls |
| --- | --- |
| | |

| Smoke Detectors | Fire Extinguishers |
| --- | --- |
| | |

# Where *it is?*

## Water Heater

## Electrical Box

## Hvac Units

## Water Meter & Min Shut-off

## Gas Meter & Maib Shut-Off

## Sprinkler Controls

## Smoke Detectors

## Fire Extinguishers

# Where *it is?*

| Water Heater | Electrical Box |
| --- | --- |
| | |

| Hvac Units | Water Meter & Min Shut-off |
| --- | --- |
| | |

| Gas Meter & Maib Shut-Off | Sprinkler Controls |
| --- | --- |
| | |

| Smoke Detectors | Fire Extinguishers |
| --- | --- |
| | |

# Where *it is?*

<table>
<tr><td>

**Water Heater**

</td><td>

**Electrical Box**

</td></tr>
<tr><td>

**Hvac Units**

</td><td>

**Water Meter & Min Shut-off**

</td></tr>
<tr><td>

**Gas Meter & Maib Shut-Off**

</td><td>

**Sprinkler Controls**

</td></tr>
<tr><td>

**Smoke Detectors**

</td><td>

**Fire Extinguishers**

</td></tr>
</table>

# Where *it is?*

| Water Heater | Electrical Box |
| --- | --- |
| | |

| Hvac Units | Water Meter & Min Shut-off |
| --- | --- |
| | |

| Gas Meter & Maib Shut-Off | Sprinkler Controls |
| --- | --- |
| | |

| Smoke Detectors | Fire Extinguishers |
| --- | --- |
| | |

# Where *it is?*

| **Water Heater** | **Electrical Box** |
|---|---|
| | |

| **Hvac Units** | **Water Meter & Min Shut-off** |
|---|---|
| | |

| **Gas Meter & Maib Shut-Off** | **Sprinkler Controls** |
|---|---|
| | |

| **Smoke Detectors** | **Fire Extinguishers** |
|---|---|
| | |

# Where *it is?*

| Water Heater | Electrical Box |
|---|---|
| | |

| Hvac Units | Water Meter & Min Shut-off |
|---|---|
| | |

| Gas Meter & Maib Shut-Off | Sprinkler Controls |
|---|---|
| | |

| Smoke Detectors | Fire Extinguishers |
|---|---|
| | |

# Where *it is?*

| Water Heater | Electrical Box |
|---|---|
|  |  |

| Hvac Units | Water Meter & Min Shut-off |
|---|---|
|  |  |

| Gas Meter & Maib Shut-Off | Sprinkler Controls |
|---|---|
|  |  |

| Smoke Detectors | Fire Extinguishers |
|---|---|
|  |  |

# Maintenance Service *Log*

| Date | System / Appliance | Problem |
| --- | --- | --- |
|  |  |  |
|  |  |  |
|  |  |  |
|  |  |  |
|  |  |  |
|  |  |  |
|  |  |  |
|  |  |  |
|  |  |  |
|  |  |  |
|  |  |  |
|  |  |  |
|  |  |  |
|  |  |  |
|  |  |  |
|  |  |  |
|  |  |  |
|  |  |  |
|  |  |  |
|  |  |  |

# Maintenance Service *Log*

| Date | System / Appliance | Problem |
| --- | --- | --- |
|  |  |  |
|  |  |  |
|  |  |  |
|  |  |  |
|  |  |  |
|  |  |  |
|  |  |  |
|  |  |  |
|  |  |  |
|  |  |  |
|  |  |  |
|  |  |  |
|  |  |  |
|  |  |  |
|  |  |  |
|  |  |  |
|  |  |  |
|  |  |  |
|  |  |  |

# Maintenance Service *Log*

| Date | System / Appliance | Problem |
|---|---|---|
|  |  |  |
|  |  |  |
|  |  |  |
|  |  |  |
|  |  |  |
|  |  |  |
|  |  |  |
|  |  |  |
|  |  |  |
|  |  |  |
|  |  |  |
|  |  |  |
|  |  |  |
|  |  |  |
|  |  |  |
|  |  |  |
|  |  |  |
|  |  |  |
|  |  |  |

# Maintenance Service *Log*

| Date | System / Appliance | Problem |
| --- | --- | --- |
|  |  |  |
|  |  |  |
|  |  |  |
|  |  |  |
|  |  |  |
|  |  |  |
|  |  |  |
|  |  |  |
|  |  |  |
|  |  |  |
|  |  |  |
|  |  |  |
|  |  |  |
|  |  |  |
|  |  |  |
|  |  |  |
|  |  |  |
|  |  |  |
|  |  |  |
|  |  |  |
|  |  |  |

# Maintenance Service *Log*

| Date | System / Appliance | Problem |
| --- | --- | --- |
|  |  |  |
|  |  |  |
|  |  |  |
|  |  |  |
|  |  |  |
|  |  |  |
|  |  |  |
|  |  |  |
|  |  |  |
|  |  |  |
|  |  |  |
|  |  |  |
|  |  |  |
|  |  |  |
|  |  |  |
|  |  |  |
|  |  |  |
|  |  |  |
|  |  |  |
|  |  |  |
|  |  |  |

# Maintenance Service *Log*

| Date | System / Appliance | Problem |
| --- | --- | --- |
|  |  |  |
|  |  |  |
|  |  |  |
|  |  |  |
|  |  |  |
|  |  |  |
|  |  |  |
|  |  |  |
|  |  |  |
|  |  |  |
|  |  |  |
|  |  |  |
|  |  |  |
|  |  |  |
|  |  |  |
|  |  |  |
|  |  |  |
|  |  |  |
|  |  |  |
|  |  |  |

# Maintenance Service *Log*

| Date | System / Appliance | Problem |
| --- | --- | --- |
|  |  |  |

# Maintenance Service *Log*

| Date | System / Appliance | Problem |
| --- | --- | --- |
|  |  |  |
|  |  |  |
|  |  |  |
|  |  |  |
|  |  |  |
|  |  |  |
|  |  |  |
|  |  |  |
|  |  |  |
|  |  |  |
|  |  |  |
|  |  |  |
|  |  |  |
|  |  |  |
|  |  |  |
|  |  |  |
|  |  |  |
|  |  |  |
|  |  |  |
|  |  |  |
|  |  |  |

# Maintenance Service *Log*

| Date | System / Appliance | Problem |
| --- | --- | --- |
|  |  |  |
|  |  |  |
|  |  |  |
|  |  |  |
|  |  |  |
|  |  |  |
|  |  |  |
|  |  |  |
|  |  |  |
|  |  |  |
|  |  |  |
|  |  |  |
|  |  |  |
|  |  |  |
|  |  |  |
|  |  |  |
|  |  |  |
|  |  |  |
|  |  |  |
|  |  |  |
|  |  |  |

# Maintenance Service *Log*

| Date | System / Appliance | Problem |
|---|---|---|
|  |  |  |
|  |  |  |
|  |  |  |
|  |  |  |
|  |  |  |
|  |  |  |
|  |  |  |
|  |  |  |
|  |  |  |
|  |  |  |
|  |  |  |
|  |  |  |
|  |  |  |
|  |  |  |
|  |  |  |
|  |  |  |
|  |  |  |
|  |  |  |
|  |  |  |
|  |  |  |
|  |  |  |

# Maintenance Service Log

| Date | System / Appliance | Problem |
|---|---|---|
|  |  |  |
|  |  |  |
|  |  |  |
|  |  |  |
|  |  |  |
|  |  |  |
|  |  |  |
|  |  |  |
|  |  |  |
|  |  |  |
|  |  |  |
|  |  |  |
|  |  |  |
|  |  |  |
|  |  |  |
|  |  |  |
|  |  |  |
|  |  |  |
|  |  |  |
|  |  |  |
|  |  |  |

# Maintenance Service *Log*

| Date | System / Appliance | Problem |
| --- | --- | --- |
|  |  |  |
|  |  |  |
|  |  |  |
|  |  |  |
|  |  |  |
|  |  |  |
|  |  |  |
|  |  |  |
|  |  |  |
|  |  |  |
|  |  |  |
|  |  |  |
|  |  |  |
|  |  |  |
|  |  |  |
|  |  |  |
|  |  |  |
|  |  |  |
|  |  |  |
|  |  |  |
|  |  |  |
|  |  |  |

# Maintenance Service *Log*

| Date | System / Appliance | Problem |
| --- | --- | --- |
|  |  |  |
|  |  |  |
|  |  |  |
|  |  |  |
|  |  |  |
|  |  |  |
|  |  |  |
|  |  |  |
|  |  |  |
|  |  |  |
|  |  |  |
|  |  |  |
|  |  |  |
|  |  |  |
|  |  |  |
|  |  |  |
|  |  |  |
|  |  |  |
|  |  |  |
|  |  |  |
|  |  |  |
|  |  |  |
|  |  |  |
|  |  |  |
|  |  |  |

# Maintenance Service *Log*

| Date | System / Appliance | Problem |
| --- | --- | --- |
|  |  |  |
|  |  |  |
|  |  |  |
|  |  |  |
|  |  |  |
|  |  |  |
|  |  |  |
|  |  |  |
|  |  |  |
|  |  |  |
|  |  |  |
|  |  |  |
|  |  |  |
|  |  |  |
|  |  |  |
|  |  |  |
|  |  |  |
|  |  |  |
|  |  |  |
|  |  |  |

# Maintenance Service *Log*

| Date | System / Appliance | Problem |
| --- | --- | --- |
|  |  |  |
|  |  |  |
|  |  |  |
|  |  |  |
|  |  |  |
|  |  |  |
|  |  |  |
|  |  |  |
|  |  |  |
|  |  |  |
|  |  |  |
|  |  |  |
|  |  |  |
|  |  |  |
|  |  |  |
|  |  |  |
|  |  |  |
|  |  |  |
|  |  |  |
|  |  |  |
|  |  |  |
|  |  |  |

# Maintenance Service *Log*

| Date | System / Appliance | Problem |
| --- | --- | --- |
|  |  |  |
|  |  |  |
|  |  |  |
|  |  |  |
|  |  |  |
|  |  |  |
|  |  |  |
|  |  |  |
|  |  |  |
|  |  |  |
|  |  |  |
|  |  |  |
|  |  |  |
|  |  |  |
|  |  |  |
|  |  |  |
|  |  |  |
|  |  |  |
|  |  |  |
|  |  |  |
|  |  |  |

# Maintenance Service *Log*

| Date | System / Appliance | Problem |
| --- | --- | --- |
|  |  |  |
|  |  |  |
|  |  |  |
|  |  |  |
|  |  |  |
|  |  |  |
|  |  |  |
|  |  |  |
|  |  |  |
|  |  |  |
|  |  |  |
|  |  |  |
|  |  |  |
|  |  |  |
|  |  |  |
|  |  |  |
|  |  |  |
|  |  |  |
|  |  |  |
|  |  |  |
|  |  |  |
|  |  |  |
|  |  |  |
|  |  |  |

# Maintenance Service *Log*

| Date | System / Appliance | Problem |
| --- | --- | --- |
|  |  |  |
|  |  |  |
|  |  |  |
|  |  |  |
|  |  |  |
|  |  |  |
|  |  |  |
|  |  |  |
|  |  |  |
|  |  |  |
|  |  |  |
|  |  |  |
|  |  |  |
|  |  |  |
|  |  |  |
|  |  |  |
|  |  |  |
|  |  |  |
|  |  |  |
|  |  |  |
|  |  |  |

# Maintenance Service *Log*

| Date | System / Appliance | Problem |
|------|--------------------|---------|
|      |                    |         |
|      |                    |         |
|      |                    |         |
|      |                    |         |
|      |                    |         |
|      |                    |         |
|      |                    |         |
|      |                    |         |
|      |                    |         |
|      |                    |         |
|      |                    |         |
|      |                    |         |
|      |                    |         |
|      |                    |         |
|      |                    |         |
|      |                    |         |
|      |                    |         |
|      |                    |         |

# Maintenance Service *Log*

| Date | System / Appliance | Problem |
|------|-------------------|---------|
|      |                    |         |
|      |                    |         |
|      |                    |         |
|      |                    |         |
|      |                    |         |
|      |                    |         |
|      |                    |         |
|      |                    |         |
|      |                    |         |
|      |                    |         |
|      |                    |         |
|      |                    |         |
|      |                    |         |
|      |                    |         |
|      |                    |         |
|      |                    |         |
|      |                    |         |
|      |                    |         |
|      |                    |         |
|      |                    |         |
|      |                    |         |

# Maintenance Service *Log*

| Date | System / Appliance | Problem |
| --- | --- | --- |
|  |  |  |
|  |  |  |
|  |  |  |
|  |  |  |
|  |  |  |
|  |  |  |
|  |  |  |
|  |  |  |
|  |  |  |
|  |  |  |
|  |  |  |
|  |  |  |
|  |  |  |
|  |  |  |
|  |  |  |
|  |  |  |
|  |  |  |
|  |  |  |
|  |  |  |
|  |  |  |
|  |  |  |

# Maintenance Service *Log*

| Date | System / Appliance | Problem |
| --- | --- | --- |
|  |  |  |
|  |  |  |
|  |  |  |
|  |  |  |
|  |  |  |
|  |  |  |
|  |  |  |
|  |  |  |
|  |  |  |
|  |  |  |
|  |  |  |
|  |  |  |
|  |  |  |
|  |  |  |
|  |  |  |
|  |  |  |
|  |  |  |
|  |  |  |
|  |  |  |
|  |  |  |
|  |  |  |

# Maintenance Service *Log*

| Date | System / Appliance | Problem |
| --- | --- | --- |
|  |  |  |
|  |  |  |
|  |  |  |
|  |  |  |
|  |  |  |
|  |  |  |
|  |  |  |
|  |  |  |
|  |  |  |
|  |  |  |
|  |  |  |
|  |  |  |
|  |  |  |
|  |  |  |
|  |  |  |
|  |  |  |
|  |  |  |
|  |  |  |
|  |  |  |

# Maintenance Service *Log*

| Date | System / Appliance | Problem |
| --- | --- | --- |
|  |  |  |
|  |  |  |
|  |  |  |
|  |  |  |
|  |  |  |
|  |  |  |
|  |  |  |
|  |  |  |
|  |  |  |
|  |  |  |
|  |  |  |
|  |  |  |
|  |  |  |
|  |  |  |
|  |  |  |
|  |  |  |
|  |  |  |
|  |  |  |
|  |  |  |
|  |  |  |
|  |  |  |

| Contrac Phone | How Was It Resolved | Satisfaction Rating |
| --- | --- | --- |
|  |  |  |
|  |  |  |
|  |  |  |
|  |  |  |
|  |  |  |
|  |  |  |
|  |  |  |
|  |  |  |
|  |  |  |
|  |  |  |
|  |  |  |
|  |  |  |
|  |  |  |
|  |  |  |
|  |  |  |
|  |  |  |
|  |  |  |
|  |  |  |
|  |  |  |

| Contrac Phone | How Was It Resolved | Satisfaction Rating |
| --- | --- | --- |
|  |  |  |
|  |  |  |
|  |  |  |

| Contrac Phone | How Was It Resolved | Satisfaction Rating |
| --- | --- | --- |
|  |  |  |
|  |  |  |
|  |  |  |
|  |  |  |
|  |  |  |
|  |  |  |
|  |  |  |
|  |  |  |
|  |  |  |
|  |  |  |
|  |  |  |
|  |  |  |
|  |  |  |
|  |  |  |
|  |  |  |
|  |  |  |
|  |  |  |
|  |  |  |
|  |  |  |
|  |  |  |
|  |  |  |
|  |  |  |
|  |  |  |
|  |  |  |

| Contrac Phone | How Was It Resolved | Satisfaction Rating |
| --- | --- | --- |
|  |  |  |
|  |  |  |
|  |  |  |
|  |  |  |
|  |  |  |
|  |  |  |
|  |  |  |
|  |  |  |
|  |  |  |
|  |  |  |
|  |  |  |
|  |  |  |
|  |  |  |
|  |  |  |
|  |  |  |
|  |  |  |
|  |  |  |
|  |  |  |
|  |  |  |
|  |  |  |
|  |  |  |
|  |  |  |
|  |  |  |

| Contrac Phone | How Was It Resolved | Satisfaction Rating |
| --- | --- | --- |
| | | |
| | | |
| | | |
| | | |
| | | |
| | | |
| | | |
| | | |
| | | |
| | | |
| | | |
| | | |
| | | |
| | | |
| | | |
| | | |
| | | |
| | | |
| | | |
| | | |
| | | |
| | | |

| Contrac Phone | How Was It Resolved | Satisfaction Rating |
| --- | --- | --- |
|  |  |  |
|  |  |  |
|  |  |  |
|  |  |  |
|  |  |  |
|  |  |  |
|  |  |  |
|  |  |  |
|  |  |  |
|  |  |  |
|  |  |  |
|  |  |  |
|  |  |  |
|  |  |  |
|  |  |  |
|  |  |  |
|  |  |  |
| Contrac Phone | How Was It Resolved | Satisfaction Rating |
|  |  |  |
|  |  |  |
|  |  |  |

| Contrac Phone | How Was It Resolved | Satisfaction Rating |
| --- | --- | --- |
|  |  |  |
|  |  |  |
|  |  |  |
|  |  |  |
|  |  |  |
|  |  |  |
|  |  |  |
|  |  |  |
|  |  |  |
|  |  |  |
|  |  |  |
|  |  |  |
|  |  |  |
|  |  |  |
|  |  |  |
|  |  |  |
|  |  |  |
|  |  |  |
|  |  |  |
|  |  |  |
|  |  |  |
|  |  |  |
|  |  |  |
|  |  |  |

| Contrac Phone | How Was It Resolved | Satisfaction Rating |
| --- | --- | --- |
|  |  |  |
|  |  |  |
|  |  |  |
|  |  |  |
|  |  |  |
|  |  |  |
|  |  |  |
|  |  |  |
|  |  |  |
|  |  |  |
|  |  |  |
|  |  |  |
|  |  |  |
|  |  |  |
|  |  |  |
|  |  |  |
|  |  |  |
|  |  |  |
|  |  |  |
|  |  |  |
|  |  |  |
|  |  |  |
|  |  |  |
|  |  |  |

| Contrac Phone | How Was It Resolved | Satisfaction Rating |
| --- | --- | --- |
|  |  |  |
|  |  |  |
|  |  |  |
|  |  |  |
|  |  |  |
|  |  |  |
|  |  |  |
|  |  |  |
|  |  |  |
|  |  |  |
|  |  |  |
|  |  |  |
|  |  |  |
|  |  |  |
|  |  |  |
|  |  |  |
|  |  |  |
|  |  |  |
|  |  |  |
|  |  |  |
|  |  |  |
|  |  |  |

| Contrac Phone | How Was It Resolved | Satisfaction Rating |
| --- | --- | --- |
| | | |
| | | |
| | | |
| | | |
| | | |
| | | |
| | | |
| | | |
| | | |
| | | |
| | | |
| | | |
| | | |
| | | |
| | | |
| | | |
| | | |
| | | |

| Contrac Phone | How Was It Resolved | Satisfaction Rating |
| --- | --- | --- |
| | | |
| | | |
| | | |

| Contrac Phone | How Was It Resolved | Satisfaction Rating |
| --- | --- | --- |
|  |  |  |
|  |  |  |
|  |  |  |
|  |  |  |
|  |  |  |
|  |  |  |
|  |  |  |
|  |  |  |
|  |  |  |
|  |  |  |
|  |  |  |
|  |  |  |
|  |  |  |
|  |  |  |
|  |  |  |
|  |  |  |
|  |  |  |
|  |  |  |
|  |  |  |
|  |  |  |
|  |  |  |
|  |  |  |
|  |  |  |

| Contrac Phone | How Was It Resolved | Satisfaction Rating |
| --- | --- | --- |
|  |  |  |
|  |  |  |
|  |  |  |
|  |  |  |
|  |  |  |
|  |  |  |
|  |  |  |
|  |  |  |
|  |  |  |
|  |  |  |
|  |  |  |
|  |  |  |
|  |  |  |
|  |  |  |
|  |  |  |
|  |  |  |
|  |  |  |
|  |  |  |
|  |  |  |
|  |  |  |

| Contrac Phone | How Was It Resolved | Satisfaction Rating |
| --- | --- | --- |
|  |  |  |
|  |  |  |
|  |  |  |
|  |  |  |
|  |  |  |
|  |  |  |
|  |  |  |
|  |  |  |
|  |  |  |
|  |  |  |
|  |  |  |
|  |  |  |
|  |  |  |
|  |  |  |
|  |  |  |
|  |  |  |
|  |  |  |
|  |  |  |
|  |  |  |
|  |  |  |
|  |  |  |
|  |  |  |

| Contrac Phone | How Was It Resolved | Satisfaction Rating |
| --- | --- | --- |
| | | |
| | | |
| | | |
| | | |
| | | |
| | | |
| | | |
| | | |
| | | |
| | | |
| | | |
| | | |
| | | |
| | | |
| | | |
| | | |
| | | |
| | | |
| | | |
| | | |
| | | |
| | | |
| | | |

| Contrac Phone | How Was It Resolved | Satisfaction Rating |
| --- | --- | --- |
| | | |
| | | |

| Contrac Phone | How Was It Resolved | Satisfaction Rating |
| --- | --- | --- |
|  |  |  |
|  |  |  |
|  |  |  |
|  |  |  |
|  |  |  |
|  |  |  |
|  |  |  |
|  |  |  |
|  |  |  |
|  |  |  |
|  |  |  |
|  |  |  |
|  |  |  |
|  |  |  |
|  |  |  |
|  |  |  |
|  |  |  |
|  |  |  |
|  |  |  |

| Contrac Phone | How Was It Resolved | Satisfaction Rating |
| --- | --- | --- |
|  |  |  |
|  |  |  |
|  |  |  |
|  |  |  |
|  |  |  |
|  |  |  |
|  |  |  |
|  |  |  |
|  |  |  |
|  |  |  |
|  |  |  |
|  |  |  |
|  |  |  |
|  |  |  |
|  |  |  |
|  |  |  |
|  |  |  |
|  |  |  |
|  |  |  |

| Contrac Phone | How Was It Resolved | Satisfaction Rating |
| --- | --- | --- |
|  |  |  |
|  |  |  |
|  |  |  |
|  |  |  |
|  |  |  |
|  |  |  |
|  |  |  |
|  |  |  |
|  |  |  |
|  |  |  |
|  |  |  |
|  |  |  |
|  |  |  |
|  |  |  |
|  |  |  |
|  |  |  |
|  |  |  |
|  |  |  |
|  |  |  |
|  |  |  |
|  |  |  |
|  |  |  |
|  |  |  |

| Contrac Phone | How Was It Resolved | Satisfaction Rating |
| --- | --- | --- |
| | | |
| | | |
| | | |
| | | |
| | | |
| | | |
| | | |
| | | |
| | | |
| | | |
| | | |
| | | |
| | | |
| | | |
| | | |
| | | |
| | | |
| | | |
| | | |

| Contrac Phone | How Was It Resolved | Satisfaction Rating |
| --- | --- | --- |
|  |  |  |
|  |  |  |
|  |  |  |
|  |  |  |
|  |  |  |
|  |  |  |
|  |  |  |
|  |  |  |
|  |  |  |
|  |  |  |
|  |  |  |
|  |  |  |
|  |  |  |
|  |  |  |
|  |  |  |
|  |  |  |
|  |  |  |
|  |  |  |
|  |  |  |
|  |  |  |
|  |  |  |
|  |  |  |

| Contrac Phone | How Was It Resolved | Satisfaction Rating |
| --- | --- | --- |
|  |  |  |
|  |  |  |
|  |  |  |
|  |  |  |
|  |  |  |
|  |  |  |
|  |  |  |
|  |  |  |
|  |  |  |
|  |  |  |
|  |  |  |
|  |  |  |
|  |  |  |
|  |  |  |
|  |  |  |
|  |  |  |
|  |  |  |
|  |  |  |
|  |  |  |
|  |  |  |

| Contrac Phone | How Was It Resolved | Satisfaction Rating |
| --- | --- | --- |
|  |  |  |
|  |  |  |
|  |  |  |
|  |  |  |
|  |  |  |
|  |  |  |
|  |  |  |
|  |  |  |
|  |  |  |
|  |  |  |
|  |  |  |
|  |  |  |
|  |  |  |
|  |  |  |
|  |  |  |
|  |  |  |
|  |  |  |
|  |  |  |
|  |  |  |
|  |  |  |
|  |  |  |
|  |  |  |
|  |  |  |
|  |  |  |

| Contrac Phone | How Was It Resolved | Satisfaction Rating |
| --- | --- | --- |
|  |  |  |
|  |  |  |
|  |  |  |
|  |  |  |
|  |  |  |
|  |  |  |
|  |  |  |
|  |  |  |
|  |  |  |
|  |  |  |
|  |  |  |
|  |  |  |
|  |  |  |
|  |  |  |
|  |  |  |
|  |  |  |
| Contrac Phone | How Was It Resolved | Satisfaction Rating |
|  |  |  |
|  |  |  |
|  |  |  |

| Contrac Phone | How Was It Resolved | Satisfaction Rating |
| --- | --- | --- |
|  |  |  |
|  |  |  |
|  |  |  |
|  |  |  |
|  |  |  |
|  |  |  |
|  |  |  |
|  |  |  |
|  |  |  |
|  |  |  |
|  |  |  |
|  |  |  |
|  |  |  |
|  |  |  |
|  |  |  |
|  |  |  |
|  |  |  |
|  |  |  |
|  |  |  |
|  |  |  |
|  |  |  |
|  |  |  |

| Contrac Phone | How Was It Resolved | Satisfaction Rating |
| --- | --- | --- |
|  |  |  |
|  |  |  |
|  |  |  |
|  |  |  |
|  |  |  |
|  |  |  |
|  |  |  |
|  |  |  |
|  |  |  |
|  |  |  |
|  |  |  |
|  |  |  |
|  |  |  |
|  |  |  |
|  |  |  |
|  |  |  |
|  |  |  |
|  |  |  |
|  |  |  |
|  |  |  |
|  |  |  |
|  |  |  |
|  |  |  |
|  |  |  |

| Contrac Phone | How Was It Resolved | Satisfaction Rating |
| --- | --- | --- |
|  |  |  |
|  |  |  |
|  |  |  |
|  |  |  |
|  |  |  |
|  |  |  |
|  |  |  |
|  |  |  |
|  |  |  |
|  |  |  |
|  |  |  |
|  |  |  |
|  |  |  |
|  |  |  |
|  |  |  |
|  |  |  |
|  |  |  |
|  |  |  |
|  |  |  |
|  |  |  |

| Contrac Phone | How Was It Resolved | Satisfaction Rating |
| --- | --- | --- |
|  |  |  |
|  |  |  |
|  |  |  |
|  |  |  |
|  |  |  |
|  |  |  |
|  |  |  |
|  |  |  |
|  |  |  |
|  |  |  |
|  |  |  |
|  |  |  |
|  |  |  |
|  |  |  |
|  |  |  |
|  |  |  |
|  |  |  |
|  |  |  |
|  |  |  |

| Contrac Phone | How Was It Resolved | Satisfaction Rating |
| --- | --- | --- |
|  |  |  |
|  |  |  |
|  |  |  |
|  |  |  |
|  |  |  |
|  |  |  |
|  |  |  |
|  |  |  |
|  |  |  |
|  |  |  |
|  |  |  |
|  |  |  |
|  |  |  |
|  |  |  |
|  |  |  |
|  |  |  |
|  |  |  |
|  |  |  |
|  |  |  |
|  |  |  |
|  |  |  |
|  |  |  |
|  |  |  |

| Contrac Phone | How Was It Resolved | Satisfaction Rating |
| --- | --- | --- |
|  |  |  |
|  |  |  |
|  |  |  |
|  |  |  |
|  |  |  |
|  |  |  |
|  |  |  |
|  |  |  |
|  |  |  |
|  |  |  |
|  |  |  |
|  |  |  |
|  |  |  |
|  |  |  |
|  |  |  |
|  |  |  |
| Contrac Phone | How Was It Resolved | Satisfaction Rating |
|  |  |  |
|  |  |  |
|  |  |  |

| Contrac Phone | How Was It Resolved | Satisfaction Rating |
|---|---|---|
|  |  |  |
|  |  |  |
|  |  |  |
|  |  |  |
|  |  |  |
|  |  |  |
|  |  |  |
|  |  |  |
|  |  |  |
|  |  |  |
|  |  |  |
|  |  |  |
|  |  |  |
|  |  |  |
|  |  |  |
|  |  |  |
|  |  |  |
|  |  |  |
|  |  |  |
|  |  |  |
|  |  |  |
|  |  |  |
|  |  |  |
|  |  |  |

| Contrac Phone | How Was It Resolved | Satisfaction Rating |
| --- | --- | --- |
|  |  |  |
|  |  |  |
|  |  |  |
|  |  |  |
|  |  |  |
|  |  |  |
|  |  |  |
|  |  |  |
|  |  |  |
|  |  |  |
|  |  |  |
| Contrac Phone | How Was It Resolved | Satisfaction Rating |
|  |  |  |
|  |  |  |
|  |  |  |

| Contrac Phone | How Was It Resolved | Satisfaction Rating |
| --- | --- | --- |
|  |  |  |
|  |  |  |
|  |  |  |
|  |  |  |
|  |  |  |
|  |  |  |
|  |  |  |
|  |  |  |
|  |  |  |
|  |  |  |
|  |  |  |
|  |  |  |
|  |  |  |
|  |  |  |
|  |  |  |
|  |  |  |
|  |  |  |
|  |  |  |
|  |  |  |
|  |  |  |
|  |  |  |
|  |  |  |

| Contrac Phone | How Was It Resolved | Satisfaction Rating |
|---|---|---|
|  |  |  |
|  |  |  |
|  |  |  |
|  |  |  |
|  |  |  |
|  |  |  |
|  |  |  |
|  |  |  |
|  |  |  |
|  |  |  |
|  |  |  |
|  |  |  |
|  |  |  |
|  |  |  |
|  |  |  |
|  |  |  |
|  |  |  |
|  |  |  |
|  |  |  |

| Contrac Phone | How Was It Resolved | Satisfaction Rating |
| --- | --- | --- |
|  |  |  |
|  |  |  |
|  |  |  |
|  |  |  |
|  |  |  |
|  |  |  |
|  |  |  |
|  |  |  |
|  |  |  |
|  |  |  |
|  |  |  |
|  |  |  |
|  |  |  |
|  |  |  |
|  |  |  |
|  |  |  |
|  |  |  |
|  |  |  |
|  |  |  |
|  |  |  |
|  |  |  |
|  |  |  |

| Contrac Phone | How Was It Resolved | Satisfaction Rating |
| --- | --- | --- |
|  |  |  |
|  |  |  |
|  |  |  |
|  |  |  |
|  |  |  |
|  |  |  |
|  |  |  |
|  |  |  |
|  |  |  |
|  |  |  |
|  |  |  |
|  |  |  |
|  |  |  |
|  |  |  |
|  |  |  |
|  |  |  |
|  |  |  |
|  |  |  |
|  |  |  |
|  |  |  |
|  |  |  |
|  |  |  |
|  |  |  |
|  |  |  |

| Contrac Phone | How Was It Resolved | Satisfaction Rating |
| --- | --- | --- |
|  |  |  |
|  |  |  |
|  |  |  |
|  |  |  |
|  |  |  |
|  |  |  |
|  |  |  |
|  |  |  |
|  |  |  |
|  |  |  |
|  |  |  |
|  |  |  |
|  |  |  |
|  |  |  |
|  |  |  |
|  |  |  |
|  |  |  |
|  |  |  |
|  |  |  |
|  |  |  |
|  |  |  |
|  |  |  |

| Contrac Phone | How Was It Resolved | Satisfaction Rating |
| --- | --- | --- |
|  |  |  |
|  |  |  |
|  |  |  |
|  |  |  |
|  |  |  |
|  |  |  |
|  |  |  |
|  |  |  |
|  |  |  |
|  |  |  |
|  |  |  |
|  |  |  |
|  |  |  |
|  |  |  |
|  |  |  |
|  |  |  |
|  |  |  |
|  |  |  |
|  |  |  |
|  |  |  |
|  |  |  |
|  |  |  |
|  |  |  |

| Contrac Phone | How Was It Resolved | Satisfaction Rating |
| --- | --- | --- |
|  |  |  |
|  |  |  |
|  |  |  |
|  |  |  |
|  |  |  |
|  |  |  |
|  |  |  |
|  |  |  |
|  |  |  |
|  |  |  |
|  |  |  |
|  |  |  |
|  |  |  |
|  |  |  |
|  |  |  |
|  |  |  |
|  |  |  |
|  |  |  |
|  |  |  |
|  |  |  |
|  |  |  |
|  |  |  |
|  |  |  |

# Project *Planner*

**Name Of Project**

**Project Description :**

**Completion Date**     **Total Budget**

| Materials List | Expented Cost | Actual Cost |
| --- | --- | --- |
| | | |
| | | |
| | | |
| | | |
| | | |
| | | |
| | | |
| | | |
| | | |
| | | |
| | | |
| **Total Cost** | | |

| Services | Expented Cost | Actual Cost |
| --- | --- | --- |
| | | |
| | | |
| | | |
| | | |
| | | |
| | | |
| | | |
| | | |
| | | |
| | | |
| | | |
| **Total Cost** | | |

**Project Notes :**

# Project *Planner*

**Name Of Project**

**Project Description :**

**Completion Date** | **Total Budget**

| Materials List | Expented Cost | Actual Cost |
| --- | --- | --- |
|  |  |  |
|  |  |  |
|  |  |  |
|  |  |  |
|  |  |  |
|  |  |  |
|  |  |  |
|  |  |  |
|  |  |  |
|  |  |  |
| **Total Cost** |  |  |

| Services | Expented Cost | Actual Cos |
| --- | --- | --- |
|  |  |  |
|  |  |  |
|  |  |  |
|  |  |  |
|  |  |  |
|  |  |  |
|  |  |  |
|  |  |  |
|  |  |  |
|  |  |  |
| **Total Cost** |  |  |

**Project Notes :**

# Project *Planner*

**Name Of Project**

**Project Description :**

**Completion Date**  **Total Budget**

| Materials List | Expented Cost | Actual Cost |
| --- | --- | --- |
|  |  |  |
|  |  |  |
|  |  |  |
|  |  |  |
|  |  |  |
|  |  |  |
|  |  |  |
|  |  |  |
|  |  |  |
|  |  |  |
|  |  |  |
|  |  |  |
| **Total Cost** |  |  |

| Services | Expented Cost | Actual Cost |
| --- | --- | --- |
|  |  |  |
|  |  |  |
|  |  |  |
|  |  |  |
|  |  |  |
|  |  |  |
|  |  |  |
|  |  |  |
|  |  |  |
|  |  |  |
|  |  |  |
|  |  |  |
| **Total Cost** |  |  |

**Project Notes :**

# Project *Planner*

**Name Of Project**

**Project Description :**

**Completion Date**

**Total Budget**

| Materials List | Expented Cost | Actual Cost |
|---|---|---|
|  |  |  |
|  |  |  |
|  |  |  |
|  |  |  |
|  |  |  |
|  |  |  |
|  |  |  |
|  |  |  |
|  |  |  |
|  |  |  |
|  |  |  |
| **Total Cost** |  |  |

| Services | Expented Cost | Actual Cost |
|---|---|---|
|  |  |  |
|  |  |  |
|  |  |  |
|  |  |  |
|  |  |  |
|  |  |  |
|  |  |  |
|  |  |  |
|  |  |  |
|  |  |  |
|  |  |  |
| **Total Cost** |  |  |

**Project Notes :**

# Project *Planner*

**Name Of Project**

**Project Description :**

**Completion Date**     **Total Budget**

| Materials List | Expented Cost | Actual Cost | | Services | Expented Cost | Actual Cost |
| --- | --- | --- | --- | --- | --- | --- |
| | | | | | | |
| | | | | | | |
| | | | | | | |
| | | | | | | |
| | | | | | | |
| | | | | | | |
| | | | | | | |
| | | | | | | |
| | | | | | | |
| | | | | | | |
| **Total Cost** | | | | **Total Cost** | | |

**Project Notes :**

# Project *Planner*

**Name Of Project**

**Project Description :**

**Completion Date**

**Total Budget**

| Materials List | Expented Cost | Actual Cost |
| --- | --- | --- |
|  |  |  |
|  |  |  |
|  |  |  |
|  |  |  |
|  |  |  |
|  |  |  |
|  |  |  |
|  |  |  |
|  |  |  |
|  |  |  |
|  |  |  |
| **Total Cost** |  |  |

| Services | Expented Cost | Actual Cost |
| --- | --- | --- |
|  |  |  |
|  |  |  |
|  |  |  |
|  |  |  |
|  |  |  |
|  |  |  |
|  |  |  |
|  |  |  |
|  |  |  |
|  |  |  |
|  |  |  |
| **Total Cost** |  |  |

**Project Notes :**

# Project *Planner*

**Name Of Project**

**Project Description :**

**Completion Date**    **Total Budget**

| Materials List | Expented Cost | Actual Cost |
| --- | --- | --- |
|  |  |  |
|  |  |  |
|  |  |  |
|  |  |  |
|  |  |  |
|  |  |  |
|  |  |  |
|  |  |  |
|  |  |  |
|  |  |  |
|  |  |  |
| **Total Cost** |  |  |

| Services | Expented Cost | Actual Cost |
| --- | --- | --- |
|  |  |  |
|  |  |  |
|  |  |  |
|  |  |  |
|  |  |  |
|  |  |  |
|  |  |  |
|  |  |  |
|  |  |  |
|  |  |  |
|  |  |  |
| **Total Cost** |  |  |

**Project Notes :**

# Project *Planner*

**Name Of Project**

**Project Description :**

**Completion Date**

**Total Budget**

| Materials List | Expented Cost | Actual Cost |
| --- | --- | --- |
| | | |
| | | |
| | | |
| | | |
| | | |
| | | |
| | | |
| | | |
| | | |
| | | |
| | | |
| **Total Cost** | | |

| Services | Expented Cost | Actual Cost |
| --- | --- | --- |
| | | |
| | | |
| | | |
| | | |
| | | |
| | | |
| | | |
| | | |
| | | |
| | | |
| | | |
| **Total Cost** | | |

**Project Notes :**

# Project *Planner*

**Name Of Project**

**Project Description :**

**Completion Date**     **Total Budget**

| Materials List | Expented Cost | Actual Cost |
| --- | --- | --- |
|  |  |  |
|  |  |  |
|  |  |  |
|  |  |  |
|  |  |  |
|  |  |  |
|  |  |  |
|  |  |  |
|  |  |  |
|  |  |  |
|  |  |  |
| **Total Cost** |  |  |

| Services | Expented Cost | Actual Cost |
| --- | --- | --- |
|  |  |  |
|  |  |  |
|  |  |  |
|  |  |  |
|  |  |  |
|  |  |  |
|  |  |  |
|  |  |  |
|  |  |  |
|  |  |  |
|  |  |  |
| **Total Cost** |  |  |

**Project Notes :**

# Project *Planner*

**Name Of Project**

**Project Description :**

**Completion Date**    **Total Budget**

| Materials List | Expented Cost | Actual Cost |
| --- | --- | --- |
|  |  |  |
|  |  |  |
|  |  |  |
|  |  |  |
|  |  |  |
|  |  |  |
|  |  |  |
|  |  |  |
|  |  |  |
|  |  |  |
|  |  |  |
| **Total Cost** |  |  |

| Services | Expented Cost | Actual Cost |
| --- | --- | --- |
|  |  |  |
|  |  |  |
|  |  |  |
|  |  |  |
|  |  |  |
|  |  |  |
|  |  |  |
|  |  |  |
|  |  |  |
|  |  |  |
|  |  |  |
| **Total Cost** |  |  |

**Project Notes :**

# Project *Planner*

**Name Of Project**

**Project Description :**

**Completion Date**  **Total Budget**

| Materials List | Expented Cost | Actual Cost |
| --- | --- | --- |
|  |  |  |
|  |  |  |
|  |  |  |
|  |  |  |
|  |  |  |
|  |  |  |
|  |  |  |
|  |  |  |
|  |  |  |
|  |  |  |
|  |  |  |
|  |  |  |
| **Total Cost** |  |  |

| Services | Expented Cost | Actual Cost |
| --- | --- | --- |
|  |  |  |
|  |  |  |
|  |  |  |
|  |  |  |
|  |  |  |
|  |  |  |
|  |  |  |
|  |  |  |
|  |  |  |
|  |  |  |
|  |  |  |
|  |  |  |
| **Total Cost** |  |  |

**Project Notes :**

# Project *Planner*

**Name Of Project**

**Project Description :**

**Completion Date**          **Total Budget**

| Materials List | Expented Cost | Actual Cost |
|---|---|---|
|  |  |  |
|  |  |  |
|  |  |  |
|  |  |  |
|  |  |  |
|  |  |  |
|  |  |  |
|  |  |  |
|  |  |  |
|  |  |  |
|  |  |  |
| **Total Cost** |  |  |

| Services | Expented Cost | Actual Cost |
|---|---|---|
|  |  |  |
|  |  |  |
|  |  |  |
|  |  |  |
|  |  |  |
|  |  |  |
|  |  |  |
|  |  |  |
|  |  |  |
|  |  |  |
|  |  |  |
| **Total Cost** |  |  |

**Project Notes :**

# Project *Planner*

**Name Of Project**

**Project Description :**

**Completion Date**

**Total Budget**

| Materials List | Expented Cost | Actual Cost |
| --- | --- | --- |
| | | |
| | | |
| | | |
| | | |
| | | |
| | | |
| | | |
| | | |
| | | |
| | | |
| | | |
| | | |
| **Total Cost** | | |

| Services | Expented Cost | Actual Cost |
| --- | --- | --- |
| | | |
| | | |
| | | |
| | | |
| | | |
| | | |
| | | |
| | | |
| | | |
| | | |
| | | |
| | | |
| **Total Cost** | | |

**Project Notes :**

# Project *Planner*

**Name Of Project**

**Project Description :**

**Completion Date**

**Total Budget**

| Materials List | Expented Cost | Actual Cost |
| --- | --- | --- |
| | | |
| | | |
| | | |
| | | |
| | | |
| | | |
| | | |
| | | |
| | | |
| | | |
| | | |
| **Total Cost** | | |

| Services | Expented Cost | Actual Cost |
| --- | --- | --- |
| | | |
| | | |
| | | |
| | | |
| | | |
| | | |
| | | |
| | | |
| | | |
| | | |
| | | |
| **Total Cost** | | |

**Project Notes :**

# Project *Planner*

**Name Of Project**

**Project Description :**

**Completion Date**  **Total Budget**

| Materials List | Expented Cost | Actual Cost |
| --- | --- | --- |
|  |  |  |
|  |  |  |
|  |  |  |
|  |  |  |
|  |  |  |
|  |  |  |
|  |  |  |
|  |  |  |
|  |  |  |
|  |  |  |
|  |  |  |
|  |  |  |
| **Total Cost** |  |  |

| Services | Expented Cost | Actual Cost |
| --- | --- | --- |
|  |  |  |
|  |  |  |
|  |  |  |
|  |  |  |
|  |  |  |
|  |  |  |
|  |  |  |
|  |  |  |
|  |  |  |
|  |  |  |
|  |  |  |
|  |  |  |
| **Total Cost** |  |  |

**Project Notes :**

# Project *Planner*

**Name Of Project**

**Project Description :**

**Completion Date**

**Total Budget**

| Materials List | Expented Cost | Actual Cost |
| --- | --- | --- |
| | | |
| | | |
| | | |
| | | |
| | | |
| | | |
| | | |
| | | |
| | | |
| | | |
| | | |
| **Total Cost** | | |

| Services | Expented Cost | Actual Cost |
| --- | --- | --- |
| | | |
| | | |
| | | |
| | | |
| | | |
| | | |
| | | |
| | | |
| | | |
| | | |
| | | |
| **Total Cost** | | |

**Project Notes :**

# Project *Planner*

**Name Of Project**

**Project Description :**

**Completion Date**

**Total Budget**

| Materials List | Expented Cost | Actual Cost |
| --- | --- | --- |
|  |  |  |
|  |  |  |
|  |  |  |
|  |  |  |
|  |  |  |
|  |  |  |
|  |  |  |
|  |  |  |
|  |  |  |
|  |  |  |
|  |  |  |
|  |  |  |
|  |  |  |
| **Total Cost** |  |  |

| Services | Expented Cost | Actual Cost |
| --- | --- | --- |
|  |  |  |
|  |  |  |
|  |  |  |
|  |  |  |
|  |  |  |
|  |  |  |
|  |  |  |
|  |  |  |
|  |  |  |
|  |  |  |
|  |  |  |
|  |  |  |
|  |  |  |
| **Total Cost** |  |  |

**Project Notes :**

# Project *Planner*

**Name Of Project**

**Project Description :**

**Completion Date**

**Total Budget**

| Materials List | Expented Cost | Actual Cost |
| --- | --- | --- |
|  |  |  |
|  |  |  |
|  |  |  |
|  |  |  |
|  |  |  |
|  |  |  |
|  |  |  |
|  |  |  |
|  |  |  |
|  |  |  |
| **Total Cost** |  |  |

| Services | Expented Cost | Actual Cost |
| --- | --- | --- |
|  |  |  |
|  |  |  |
|  |  |  |
|  |  |  |
|  |  |  |
|  |  |  |
|  |  |  |
|  |  |  |
|  |  |  |
|  |  |  |
| **Total Cost** |  |  |

**Project Notes :**

# Project *Planner*

**Name Of Project**

**Project Description :**

**Completion Date**          **Total Budget**

| Materials List | Expented Cost | Actual Cost |
| --- | --- | --- |
|  |  |  |
|  |  |  |
|  |  |  |
|  |  |  |
|  |  |  |
|  |  |  |
|  |  |  |
|  |  |  |
|  |  |  |
|  |  |  |
|  |  |  |
|  |  |  |
|  |  |  |
| **Total Cost** |  |  |

| Services | Expented Cost | Actual Cost |
| --- | --- | --- |
|  |  |  |
|  |  |  |
|  |  |  |
|  |  |  |
|  |  |  |
|  |  |  |
|  |  |  |
|  |  |  |
|  |  |  |
|  |  |  |
|  |  |  |
|  |  |  |
|  |  |  |
| **Total Cost** |  |  |

**Project Notes :**

# Project *Planner*

**Name Of Project**

**Project Description :**

**Completion Date**

**Total Budget**

| Materials List | Expented Cost | Actual Cost |
| --- | --- | --- |
| | | |
| | | |
| | | |
| | | |
| | | |
| | | |
| | | |
| | | |
| | | |
| | | |
| | | |
| **Total Cost** | | |

| Services | Expented Cost | Actual Cost |
| --- | --- | --- |
| | | |
| | | |
| | | |
| | | |
| | | |
| | | |
| | | |
| | | |
| | | |
| | | |
| | | |
| **Total Cost** | | |

**Project Notes :**

# Project *Planner*

**Name Of Project**

**Project Description :**

**Completion Date**          **Total Budget**

| Materials List | Expented Cost | Actual Cost |
|---|---|---|
|  |  |  |
|  |  |  |
|  |  |  |
|  |  |  |
|  |  |  |
|  |  |  |
|  |  |  |
|  |  |  |
|  |  |  |
|  |  |  |
|  |  |  |
|  |  |  |
|  |  |  |
|  |  |  |
| **Total Cost** |  |  |

| Services | Expented Cost | Actual Cost |
|---|---|---|
|  |  |  |
|  |  |  |
|  |  |  |
|  |  |  |
|  |  |  |
|  |  |  |
|  |  |  |
|  |  |  |
|  |  |  |
|  |  |  |
|  |  |  |
|  |  |  |
|  |  |  |
|  |  |  |
| **Total Cost** |  |  |

**Project Notes :**

# Project *Planner*

**Name Of Project**

**Project Description :**

**Completion Date**     **Total Budget**

| Materials List | Expented Cost | Actual Cost |
| --- | --- | --- |
|  |  |  |
|  |  |  |
|  |  |  |
|  |  |  |
|  |  |  |
|  |  |  |
|  |  |  |
|  |  |  |
|  |  |  |
|  |  |  |
|  |  |  |
| **Total Cost** |  |  |

| Services | Expented Cost | Actual Cost |
| --- | --- | --- |
|  |  |  |
|  |  |  |
|  |  |  |
|  |  |  |
|  |  |  |
|  |  |  |
|  |  |  |
|  |  |  |
|  |  |  |
|  |  |  |
|  |  |  |
| **Total Cost** |  |  |

**Project Notes :**

# Project *Planner*

**Name Of Project**

**Project Description :**

**Completion Date**     **Total Budget**

| Materials List | Expented Cost | Actual Cost |
| --- | --- | --- |
|  |  |  |
|  |  |  |
|  |  |  |
|  |  |  |
|  |  |  |
|  |  |  |
|  |  |  |
|  |  |  |
|  |  |  |
|  |  |  |
|  |  |  |
|  |  |  |
| **Total Cost** |  |  |

| Services | Expented Cost | Actual Cost |
| --- | --- | --- |
|  |  |  |
|  |  |  |
|  |  |  |
|  |  |  |
|  |  |  |
|  |  |  |
|  |  |  |
|  |  |  |
|  |  |  |
|  |  |  |
|  |  |  |
|  |  |  |
| **Total Cost** |  |  |

**Project Notes :**

# Project *Planner*

**Name Of Project**

**Project Description :**

**Completion Date**     **Total Budget**

| Materials List | Expented Cost | Actual Cost |
| --- | --- | --- |
|  |  |  |
|  |  |  |
|  |  |  |
|  |  |  |
|  |  |  |
|  |  |  |
|  |  |  |
|  |  |  |
|  |  |  |
|  |  |  |
|  |  |  |
| **Total Cost** |  |  |

| Services | Expented Cost | Actual Cost |
| --- | --- | --- |
|  |  |  |
|  |  |  |
|  |  |  |
|  |  |  |
|  |  |  |
|  |  |  |
|  |  |  |
|  |  |  |
|  |  |  |
|  |  |  |
|  |  |  |
| **Total Cost** |  |  |

**Project Notes :**

# Project *Planner*

**Name Of Project**

**Project Description :**

**Completion Date**  **Total Budget**

| Materials List | Expented Cost | Actual Cost |
| --- | --- | --- |
| | | |
| | | |
| | | |
| | | |
| | | |
| | | |
| | | |
| | | |
| | | |
| | | |
| | | |
| | | |
| **Total Cost** | | |

| Services | Expented Cost | Actual Cost |
| --- | --- | --- |
| | | |
| | | |
| | | |
| | | |
| | | |
| | | |
| | | |
| | | |
| | | |
| | | |
| | | |
| | | |
| **Total Cost** | | |

**Project Notes :**

# Project *Planner*

**Name Of Project**

**Project Description :**

**Completion Date**  **Total Budget**

| Materials List | Expented Cost | Actual Cost |
| --- | --- | --- |
|  |  |  |
|  |  |  |
|  |  |  |
|  |  |  |
|  |  |  |
|  |  |  |
|  |  |  |
|  |  |  |
|  |  |  |
|  |  |  |
|  |  |  |
|  |  |  |
| **Total Cost** |  |  |

| Services | Expented Cost | Actual Cost |
| --- | --- | --- |
|  |  |  |
|  |  |  |
|  |  |  |
|  |  |  |
|  |  |  |
|  |  |  |
|  |  |  |
|  |  |  |
|  |  |  |
|  |  |  |
|  |  |  |
|  |  |  |
| **Total Cost** |  |  |

**Project Notes :**

# Project *Planner*

**Name Of Project**

**Project Description :**

**Completion Date**     **Total Budget**

| Materials List | Expented Cost | Actual Cost |
| --- | --- | --- |
|  |  |  |
|  |  |  |
|  |  |  |
|  |  |  |
|  |  |  |
|  |  |  |
|  |  |  |
|  |  |  |
|  |  |  |
|  |  |  |
|  |  |  |
|  |  |  |
|  |  |  |
| **Total Cost** |  |  |

| Services | Expented Cost | Actual Cost |
| --- | --- | --- |
|  |  |  |
|  |  |  |
|  |  |  |
|  |  |  |
|  |  |  |
|  |  |  |
|  |  |  |
|  |  |  |
|  |  |  |
|  |  |  |
|  |  |  |
|  |  |  |
|  |  |  |
| **Total Cost** |  |  |

**Project Notes :**

# Project *Planner*

**Name Of Project**

**Project Description :**

**Completion Date**      **Total Budget**

| Materials List | Expented Cost | Actual Cost |
| --- | --- | --- |
|  |  |  |
|  |  |  |
|  |  |  |
|  |  |  |
|  |  |  |
|  |  |  |
|  |  |  |
|  |  |  |
|  |  |  |
|  |  |  |
|  |  |  |
| **Total Cost** |  |  |

| Services | Expented Cost | Actual Cost |
| --- | --- | --- |
|  |  |  |
|  |  |  |
|  |  |  |
|  |  |  |
|  |  |  |
|  |  |  |
|  |  |  |
|  |  |  |
|  |  |  |
|  |  |  |
|  |  |  |
| **Total Cost** |  |  |

**Project Notes :**

# Project *Planner*

**Name Of Project**

**Project Description :**

**Completion Date**     **Total Budget**

| Materials List | Expented Cost | Actual Cost |
| --- | --- | --- |
| | | |
| | | |
| | | |
| | | |
| | | |
| | | |
| | | |
| | | |
| | | |
| | | |
| | | |
| | | |
| **Total Cost** | | |

| Services | Expented Cost | Actual Cost |
| --- | --- | --- |
| | | |
| | | |
| | | |
| | | |
| | | |
| | | |
| | | |
| | | |
| | | |
| | | |
| | | |
| | | |
| **Total Cost** | | |

**Project Notes :**

# Project *Planner*

**Name Of Project**

**Project Description :**

**Completion Date**          **Total Budget**

| Materials List | Expented Cost | Actual Cost |
|---|---|---|
|  |  |  |
|  |  |  |
|  |  |  |
|  |  |  |
|  |  |  |
|  |  |  |
|  |  |  |
|  |  |  |
|  |  |  |
|  |  |  |
|  |  |  |
| **Total Cost** | | |

| Services | Expented Cost | Actual Cost |
|---|---|---|
|  |  |  |
|  |  |  |
|  |  |  |
|  |  |  |
|  |  |  |
|  |  |  |
|  |  |  |
|  |  |  |
|  |  |  |
|  |  |  |
|  |  |  |
| **Total Cost** | | |

**Project Notes :**

# Project *Planner*

**Name Of Project**

**Project Description :**

**Completion Date**

**Total Budget**

| Materials List | Expented Cost | Actual Cost |
| --- | --- | --- |
|  |  |  |
|  |  |  |
|  |  |  |
|  |  |  |
|  |  |  |
|  |  |  |
|  |  |  |
|  |  |  |
|  |  |  |
|  |  |  |
|  |  |  |
|  |  |  |
|  |  |  |
| **Total Cost** |  |  |

| Services | Expented Cost | Actual Cost |
| --- | --- | --- |
|  |  |  |
|  |  |  |
|  |  |  |
|  |  |  |
|  |  |  |
|  |  |  |
|  |  |  |
|  |  |  |
|  |  |  |
|  |  |  |
|  |  |  |
|  |  |  |
|  |  |  |
| **Total Cost** |  |  |

**Project Notes :**

# Project *Planner*

**Name Of Project**

**Project Description :**

**Completion Date**

**Total Budget**

| Materials List | Expented Cost | Actual Cost |
| --- | --- | --- |
|  |  |  |
|  |  |  |
|  |  |  |
|  |  |  |
|  |  |  |
|  |  |  |
|  |  |  |
|  |  |  |
|  |  |  |
|  |  |  |
|  |  |  |
| **Total Cost** |  |  |

| Services | Expented Cost | Actual Cost |
| --- | --- | --- |
|  |  |  |
|  |  |  |
|  |  |  |
|  |  |  |
|  |  |  |
|  |  |  |
|  |  |  |
|  |  |  |
|  |  |  |
|  |  |  |
|  |  |  |
| **Total Cost** |  |  |

**Project Notes :**

# Project *Planner*

**Name Of Project**

**Project Description :**

**Completion Date**          **Total Budget**

| Materials List | Expented Cost | Actual Cost |
|---|---|---|
|  |  |  |
|  |  |  |
|  |  |  |
|  |  |  |
|  |  |  |
|  |  |  |
|  |  |  |
|  |  |  |
|  |  |  |
|  |  |  |
|  |  |  |
|  |  |  |
| **Total Cost** |  |  |

| Services | Expented Cost | Actual Cost |
|---|---|---|
|  |  |  |
|  |  |  |
|  |  |  |
|  |  |  |
|  |  |  |
|  |  |  |
|  |  |  |
|  |  |  |
|  |  |  |
|  |  |  |
|  |  |  |
|  |  |  |
| **Total Cost** |  |  |

**Project Notes :**

# Project *Planner*

**Name Of Project**

**Project Description :**

**Completion Date**

**Total Budget**

| Materials List | Expented Cost | Actual Cost |
| --- | --- | --- |
|  |  |  |
|  |  |  |
|  |  |  |
|  |  |  |
|  |  |  |
|  |  |  |
|  |  |  |
|  |  |  |
|  |  |  |
|  |  |  |
|  |  |  |
| **Total Cost** |  |  |

| Services | Expented Cost | Actual Cost |
| --- | --- | --- |
|  |  |  |
|  |  |  |
|  |  |  |
|  |  |  |
|  |  |  |
|  |  |  |
|  |  |  |
|  |  |  |
|  |  |  |
|  |  |  |
|  |  |  |
| **Total Cost** |  |  |

**Project Notes :**

# Project *Planner*

**Name Of Project**

**Project Description :**

**Completion Date**

**Total Budget**

| Materials List | Expented Cost | Actual Cost |
| --- | --- | --- |
| | | |
| | | |
| | | |
| | | |
| | | |
| | | |
| | | |
| | | |
| | | |
| | | |
| | | |
| **Total Cost** | | |

| Services | Expented Cost | Actual Cost |
| --- | --- | --- |
| | | |
| | | |
| | | |
| | | |
| | | |
| | | |
| | | |
| | | |
| | | |
| | | |
| | | |
| **Total Cost** | | |

**Project Notes :**

# Project *Planner*

**Name Of Project**

**Project Description :**

|  |
|  |
|  |

**Completion Date** | **Total Budget**

| Materials List | Expented Cost | Actual Cost |
| --- | --- | --- |
|  |  |  |
|  |  |  |
|  |  |  |
|  |  |  |
|  |  |  |
|  |  |  |
|  |  |  |
|  |  |  |
|  |  |  |
|  |  |  |
|  |  |  |
| **Total Cost** |  |  |

| Services | Expented Cost | Actual Cost |
| --- | --- | --- |
|  |  |  |
|  |  |  |
|  |  |  |
|  |  |  |
|  |  |  |
|  |  |  |
|  |  |  |
|  |  |  |
|  |  |  |
|  |  |  |
|  |  |  |
| **Total Cost** |  |  |

**Project Notes :**

# Project *Planner*

**Name Of Project**

**Project Description :**

**Completion Date**          **Total Budget**

| Materials List | Expented Cost | Actual Cost |
| --- | --- | --- |
|  |  |  |
|  |  |  |
|  |  |  |
|  |  |  |
|  |  |  |
|  |  |  |
|  |  |  |
|  |  |  |
|  |  |  |
|  |  |  |
|  |  |  |
|  |  |  |
| **Total Cost** |  |  |

| Services | Expented Cost | Actual Cost |
| --- | --- | --- |
|  |  |  |
|  |  |  |
|  |  |  |
|  |  |  |
|  |  |  |
|  |  |  |
|  |  |  |
|  |  |  |
|  |  |  |
|  |  |  |
|  |  |  |
|  |  |  |
| **Total Cost** |  |  |

**Project Notes :**

# Project *Planner*

**Name Of Project**

**Project Description :**

**Completion Date**  **Total Budget**

| Materials List | Expented Cost | Actual Cost |
| --- | --- | --- |
|  |  |  |
|  |  |  |
|  |  |  |
|  |  |  |
|  |  |  |
|  |  |  |
|  |  |  |
|  |  |  |
|  |  |  |
|  |  |  |
| **Total Cost** |  |  |

| Services | Expented Cost | Actual Cost |
| --- | --- | --- |
|  |  |  |
|  |  |  |
|  |  |  |
|  |  |  |
|  |  |  |
|  |  |  |
|  |  |  |
|  |  |  |
|  |  |  |
|  |  |  |
| **Total Cost** |  |  |

**Project Notes :**

# Project *Planner*

**Name Of Project**

**Project Description :**

**Completion Date**     **Total Budget**

| Materials List | Expented Cost | Actual Cost |
|---|---|---|
|  |  |  |
|  |  |  |
|  |  |  |
|  |  |  |
|  |  |  |
|  |  |  |
|  |  |  |
|  |  |  |
|  |  |  |
|  |  |  |
|  |  |  |
| **Total Cost** |  |  |

| Services | Expented Cost | Actual Cost |
|---|---|---|
|  |  |  |
|  |  |  |
|  |  |  |
|  |  |  |
|  |  |  |
|  |  |  |
|  |  |  |
|  |  |  |
|  |  |  |
|  |  |  |
|  |  |  |
| **Total Cost** |  |  |

**Project Notes :**

# Project *Planner*

**Name Of Project**

**Project Description :**

**Completion Date**

**Total Budget**

| Materials List | Expented Cost | Actual Cost |
| --- | --- | --- |
| | | |
| | | |
| | | |
| | | |
| | | |
| | | |
| | | |
| | | |
| | | |
| | | |
| | | |
| **Total Cost** | | |

| Services | Expented Cost | Actual Cos |
| --- | --- | --- |
| | | |
| | | |
| | | |
| | | |
| | | |
| | | |
| | | |
| | | |
| | | |
| | | |
| | | |
| **Total Cost** | | |

**Project Notes :**

# Project *Planner*

**Name Of Project**

**Project Description :**

**Completion Date**          **Total Budget**

| Materials List | Expented Cost | Actual Cost |
| --- | --- | --- |
|  |  |  |
|  |  |  |
|  |  |  |
|  |  |  |
|  |  |  |
|  |  |  |
|  |  |  |
|  |  |  |
|  |  |  |
|  |  |  |
|  |  |  |
| **Total Cost** |  |  |

| Services | Expented Cost | Actual Cost |
| --- | --- | --- |
|  |  |  |
|  |  |  |
|  |  |  |
|  |  |  |
|  |  |  |
|  |  |  |
|  |  |  |
|  |  |  |
|  |  |  |
|  |  |  |
| **Total Cost** |  |  |

**Project Notes :**

# Project *Planner*

**Name Of Project**

**Project Description :**

**Completion Date**          **Total Budget**

| Materials List | Expented Cost | Actual Cost |
| --- | --- | --- |
|  |  |  |
|  |  |  |
|  |  |  |
|  |  |  |
|  |  |  |
|  |  |  |
|  |  |  |
|  |  |  |
|  |  |  |
|  |  |  |
|  |  |  |
| **Total Cost** |  |  |

| Services | Expented Cost | Actual Cos |
| --- | --- | --- |
|  |  |  |
|  |  |  |
|  |  |  |
|  |  |  |
|  |  |  |
|  |  |  |
|  |  |  |
|  |  |  |
|  |  |  |
|  |  |  |
|  |  |  |
| **Total Cost** |  |  |

**Project Notes :**

www.ingramcontent.com/pod-product-compliance
Lightning Source LLC
Chambersburg PA
CBHW080329030726
47593CB00010B/2938

9 781803 850931